DAVID J. BURNS

🍌🍌🍌🍌🍌

STRAIGHTENING

THE

BANANA

FIVE LESSONS WHEN RAISING CHILDREN

First published in Great Britain in 2018

by Mastersafe Limited

40, Spierbridge Road, Storrington,

West Sussex, RH20 4PG

The moral right of David Burns to be identified

as the author of this work has been asserted.

Copyright © David Burns 2018

All rights reserved.
No part of this publication may be reproduced, stored in a retrieval system or transmitted in any form or by any means electronic, mechanical, photocopying, recording or otherwise, without the prior written permission of the author.

ISBN: 978-0-9927539-8-6

Printed and bound in England.

Dedication

To Alfie.

May you always know that you are loved.

Grandad x

STRAIGHTENING THE BANANA

Contents

Acknowledgements	7
Straightening The Banana	9
Making the Choice	17
Quick March!	27
Deciding What Matters	35
The Personality Test	49
Letting Go	57
In Summary…	69
Final Thought	73
Can You Help?	83
About the Author	85
Other Titles by the Same Author	86

STRAIGHTENING THE BANANA

Acknowledgements

I find myself writing because people invariably share their stories with me and I respond with some words of encouragement, hope and kindness. It's therefore fair to say that I am indebted to all those parents and carers who open their hearts and tell me about their experiences. I am grateful for their honesty.

To those people who continue to encourage me to write and to not give up I thank you – it's you who make such a difference in my life.

I thank my family who have taught me so much about love – what it is and what it isn't.

8 STRAIGHTENING THE BANANA

STRAIGHTENING THE BANANA

STRAIGHTENING THE BANANA

Have you ever wondered, like me, why bananas are curved? They just don't fit in with all the other fruits, do they?

Sure, a pear looks like it's had an accident but most fruits have an oval or round shape. Recently I've taken to the challenge of losing weight – it's not easy and trying to reach my original weight of 7lb 3oz is just impossible. I know, we should learn to accept our bodies and realise that we're all beautiful. The thing is my wife is, well, very encouraging. "Do you need to eat that chocolate?" she'll ask. Truth is I probably feel like it when she's enjoying her favourite treat or I'm wandering around in her sweet shop. Even at home, when reaching to the back of a top shelf for a tin of peaches, I manage to find a bag of mini eggs. And they're still in date.

So, in my attempt to substitute sweets for something else I've opted for fruit. So far it's going well and I'm enjoying the hunt for new things. Yet, no matter what I try, I've not found anything like the banana. Its unusual shape sets it out from the rest and though the doctor says I ought to eat more fruit with skins I haven't mastered eating a whole one! So why is it so different and why isn't it like everything else? Why doesn't it conform?

My journey has led me to find out something unusual. You see, the bananas we buy in the supermarket start from flowers that hang down. Gradually, as the fruit develops, something amazing happens. The unorthodox banana, which grows in bunches, starts to change direction and turn upwards to point to the sky. It's not looking for the sun or the light but is growing away from the earth's gravitational pull. It literally defies gravity. Wow! Not only does it look different but it really doesn't follow the rules. It's this bending upwards that makes it curved – it just refuses to grow straight. The whole bunch changes direction and reaches for the sky.

This discovery has just got me thinking. You see, I have four children. A whole bunch of them and not one has conformed to be exactly what we thought they'd turn out to be. In fact, I'm certain that when it came to parenting and raising children the health visitor was less than truthful about the process! (She only had cats and dogs). Children are born and for the first few months things seem great. Though I wasn't keen on the sleepless nights each one of my children followed the same pattern – eat, sleep, cry, dirty the nappy, eat again, sleep, wake-up crying, dirty the nappy. They were fully dependent on the love and care my wife and I provided. Then, as the months passed something began to happen. They began to change direction. All of them, without exception, began to take interest in their surroundings and decide what they liked or didn't like. I have to admit, they continue to change even today (one is in his twenties). And therein lies the challenge to all parents – how do we cope with this change?

There are many books about parenting and I'm sometimes left wondering which volumes parents choose. Many give great advice and set out plans that tell us what to do. They're perfect when everything is going well. But what I wanted to know at times was how to parent a child through the tough times. You see, when everything in the garden is lovely, parenting a child seems easy. But what about when the banana is turning? When the child isn't going down the straight and narrow? When there's trouble? When there's a disability? When we or our children are sick? When we've suffered a bereavement? When they defy convention? What do we do?

This book is for all parents who look across their neighbour's fence and ask the question, "Why can't my kids be like theirs?" You've had some challenging times and right now you're under pressure. Everyone else's family life seems perfect (though it probably isn't) but yours is, well, just not like that. You've found parenting is demanding and it's no glide down the slide. Welcome to the real world.

For most of us, raising a child seems to be a rugged uphill climb to a peak. Sometimes we wonder whether the arrival at the summit is worth all that effort. Let me tell you something – it's worth it. You see, what I've discovered is this. I can't be responsible for all the choices my children make and neither can I map their life out for them. But I can choose to apply principles and values in our family life that will teach them a good path to tread. I can look back and say, despite all the mistakes and troubles, "I've done the best job I could with the tools I had to hand." Let's face it, children don't come with an instruction manual and even if they did, every child's guidance would be different. When that baby arrives we soon learn that our adult lives can never be the same again. Oh boy, does that take some adjustment!

Something else also becomes a reality too. When my wife and I decided to have a family, we had no conditions about who was allowed to arrive and share our lives. They didn't have to be perfect because we weren't. In fact, one of our children was unwell before she was born and had a high possibility of Down's syndrome. Though I understand many cannot continue with a pregnancy that has those sorts of risks (I'm not judging anyone), we accepted that life doesn't always give us exactly what we want. It's not always predictable and there are disappointments and sad days. But there are great days too. There are days I remember laughing so much I nearly gave myself a hernia. Not just chuckles – I mean the real laugh out loud stuff that everyone hears.

So, would you like to come with me as I share some of the things I've found useful when raising a family? I can't make the road smooth but I can at least lend you a hand as you climb the mountain. I want you to be able to look back across the valley and know you've done a great job because you invested whatever you could into your children's lives. It's not about next door's kids or trying to emulate someone else's success. It's not even about creating the 'dream' family. No, parenting is a journey that faces real challenges and the tough stuff. It's terribly messy! Oh, and along the way I'll add a good dose of humour too because every family needs to laugh together and have fun.

You'll notice that at the end of each chapter I've posed some 'mind curving' questions. They're not intended to be difficult but to help us all to allow our minds to curve like a banana towards a new or different way of thinking.

Are you ready to be encouraged? Let's go.

MAKING THE CHOICE

STRAIGHTENING THE BANANA

# MAKING THE CHOICE

A lady had become very upset because although her new-born baby was beautiful to her, everyone else said he was ugly. After a particularly tough morning of unkind words and criticism she sat on a park bench holding her baby and sobbed her eyes out.

An elderly man was passing by and noticed how upset she was and sat next to her. He tried to console her but no matter what he said the lady wouldn't stop crying enough to tell him what was wrong. The elderly man decided that he'd get her a brandy from the pub on the corner and hurried off. Fifteen minutes later he arrived back, sat next to the lady and smiled.

"Here you are, my dear. I've bought you a glass of brandy to calm you down. Oh, and here are some nuts for the monkey."

To parents, their firstborn baby is the most beautiful person in the world (you rarely get parents admitting their babies are ugly, do you?). They think he or she is wonderful and their life is complete. And rightly so. It doesn't matter what others say because this little life is just perfect – for about forty-eight hours anyway. Then reality kicks in because they've become a family and the next few years (at least eighteen) involve sacrifices from both of them. No, I don't mean they offer the baby up in some religious ritual! What I mean is they both put themselves second to the needs of the child. He or she becomes the centre of attention. Although this may come naturally to many parents, it's not always a straightforward process and things don't necessarily turn out as planned. But remember what I said - I *want you to be able to look back across the valley and know you've done a great job because you invested whatever you could into your children's lives.*

MAKING THE CHOICE

I have four children and each one is different. One boy, a girl and two non-humans isn't quite what I mean by different! They all have different personalities, different talents, different likes or dislikes and different attitudes. Two are left-handed and two are right-handed (my wife and I are both right-handed). One has dyslexia and a great sense of humour. Another has an autistic mind and is brilliant at solving puzzles. One loves art and another loves music. One is very intellectual while another is practical. Some are more sensitive than others and one is very forgetful. Some are fashion conscious while others don't seem to be bothered by the whole thing. Some are openly affectionate while others are less so. It's a very interesting family combination! They're not what we expected except that they all started out as little scrunched-up faced babies completely dependent on their mum and dad. Though there are obvious differences, do we love them all? You bet! Love is the greatest.

Love, however, has come at a cost. You might think it's easy to love a baby and it is at first. Those tiny hands and feet, that perfect nose and those beautiful eyes naturally draw your affection and wonder when you first meet. But at two in the morning when their cute little mouth is screaming blue murder for something to eat, that takes more than emotions when it comes to love. What's needed here is a decision to love no matter how tired or unwell we may feel. *That's the first lesson - I will choose to love my child because that is what is always needed.* Why do I emphasize this? My reason is simple — it's the one thing I've had to decide time and again as a parent. Things don't always go well and I have to choose love because my children need it. Love doesn't mean there's no discipline or that I'll never get cross but it does mean I'm committed to them even when they make mistakes or do things that drive me crazy. I want them to remain close, to know they are loved and that our home is a place they can feel safe.

I'd like to share with you the story of our third child because it illustrates this important lesson about a commitment to love. She was just 18 weeks old, still unborn inside the womb, when the midwife found a problem. Her little heart was being pushed over to the right-hand side by fluid that was building up inside her chest cavity. Only one lung was developing because the left one was unable to grow into the cavity that was filled with fluid. It was a terrible experience for my wife and I and we

 MAKING THE CHOICE

felt utterly powerless to do anything to fix the problem. Our little girl was ill and we couldn't hold her or comfort her because she hadn't been born. There were no previous cases the hospital could tell us about because all previous pregnancies had been ended. We truly were in the dark when it came to knowing the possible outcome. There was no hope we could cling to except to pray.

It was an emotionally challenging few weeks as doctors scanned and reviewed our daughter's heart, lungs and predicament. We were reminded on several occasions that ending the pregnancy was something we should seriously consider and that the prospects for our daughter in life were not bright. Personally, I had to consider the effect of a still birth after 40 weeks and whether it would be better to help my wife through a full labour at 22 weeks. These are not easy things to face and on top of that the doctor impressed on our minds that our daughter was six times more likely to have Down's syndrome.

Despite this there's something I remember very clearly. We were both committed to our daughter's life. It was something very personal to us and we loved her even though our eyes had never met. We had agreed that our children didn't have to be 'perfect' and that together we'd find a way to support them. Our commitment and choice to love our daughter started before she was born.

I'm so pleased to tell you that everything worked out fine. The fluid receded and our little daughter was born safely in 1997. She doesn't have Down's syndrome and she's sporty, active and does all the things the doctor's said she wouldn't. This year she turns twenty-one and it's our commitment and choice to love her before she was born and all the years after that have helped her to this point. Has it been easy sailing from birth to adulthood? Absolutely not. We've argued, cried and been frustrated. But we've also loved, encouraged and laughed a great deal and we're so blessed to have her in our lives. She recently wrote the following simple words in my Father's Day card: "To Dad, thanks for all your help and being a great dad." That means so much.

Your journey with your baby may have started before they were born and now your eyes can meet. Will you choose to love them even when your emotions feel the opposite? There are no guarantees when it comes to getting it right but

 MAKING THE CHOICE

parenting really is a lifelong commitment of love to set our children free. Even as an adult I know I'm loved and valued. And that is something I have to thank my parents for. Their continued generous encouragement and investment in my life has been the enabling force to help me explore my talents and believe there's more to come. They're still doing it and they're in their eighties!

You can do it too because love is the greatest.

MIND CURVING QUESTIONS

1. Love has many shapes and forms. Can you think of different ways people show love?
2. How does your child know you love them?
3. Love isn't always easy. How are you going to choose to love today?

STRAIGHTENING THE BANANA

QUICK MARCH!

 QUICK MARCH!

My father was in the RAF during his national service and he reminded me not to respond to every question some people ask. He had just arrived and at breakfast the first morning the officer came into the dining hall politely asking, "Any complaints? Any complaints?"

My father, being unaccustomed to the ways of the armed forces raised his hand.

"Yes Sir, I have a complaint," my father called out.

"Sergeant, this man has a complaint. Well, what seems to be the problem, private?"

"These eggs are a bit runny."

"Sergeant, he says his eggs are a bit runny?" the officer enquired.

"They do appear to be a bit runny, Sir," the sergeant agreed.

"Sergeant, we have an expert in cooking eggs. He's to report to the cook house tomorrow at 5am where he can help prepare tomorrow's breakfast. The men can look forward to perfectly cooked eggs."

My father never complained again.

Many people tried to avoid national service because the environment was, at least to begin with, harsh. Everyone was forced to conform to the service requirements and my father says it was okay provided you didn't take things personally. Some men found it difficult to cope with while others learnt to distance themselves from the emotional turmoil felt when someone barked orders and questioned their parentage.

 QUICK MARCH!

Quite a few relationships ended because it was not uncommon for girlfriends and sweethearts to find someone else nearer to home. They'd write a letter breaking everything off. My father says that it was common practice to pin these letters to a board for all to read. To support their abandoned comrade all his friends would write a letter back to the ex-girlfriend. She'd receive twenty or so letters telling her how cut up their friend has been since the break up and questioning why she could be so heartless. One thing about being in the armed forces was the comradery. Everyone stuck together because everyone was in the same situation.

It's an odd question but is there anything families can learn from the armed forces when raising a baby? It can't be the long marches up hills or the shouting of orders. These things are best left where they belong! But I think there's one thing parents can do when they start to parent a new born that comes straight out of the armed forces text book. Have you guessed what it is?

If the first lesson is to make a choice to love, the second is this*: I will introduce routine and consistency as soon as I can*. My father will tell you his time in the RAF was full of routine, from the time he got up to the time lights were turned off. Everyone knew what was expected and when. Likewise, when raising a family, I've found that introducing routine as early as possible helped all our children to be reassured, feel safe and gave my wife and I time to relax together.

Now some of you might be questioning how to do this because your situation is different. However, I want you to remember that I haven't said what the routine has to be. All our children are different and parents can decide what works best for them. We had a set evening routine of feeding, bath time and then story time. Meal times were a little hit and miss because we fed our children on demand when they were very small. However, we did introduce baths and then stories and eventually mealtimes became more of a set pattern. Though I've not set in stone which routines should be introduced, I am fairly certain which ones should not be allowed to become rooted in the family. Let me explain.

It's great to introduce things that promote family life and gives consideration to everyone. What I'm not advocating are routines that cause friction

 **QUICK MARCH!**

between parents or make life even more difficult than it is. For example, don't introduce a routine that means the child has to sleep in your bed every night because that will affect intimacy between parents. A close bond between parents is important because together they raise the family. If you're raising a family alone then it's even harder so don't introduce very late bed times because you'll get tired. What I'm encouraging here is a balance that considers the needs of parents and the needs of children. Remember you're a family and everyone is important. Parents already have to make sacrifices so starting routines that honour what has already been given up to enable parents time to relax and have their own time is, in my view, essential. It's called 'balance'. Continually running on empty is no fun and unsustainable.

There's no hard-set rule but do you see what I'm getting at? Routines that help the family to work well together are great. Routines that cause stress, difficulties and problems in the long term are not so brilliant. Ask yourself the question, "Is this helping family life to run well or is it tripping us up?" Your answer will help you to find what works well for everyone.

MIND CURVING QUESTIONS

1. What routines did you have when you were a child and have you carried them on?
2. What routines could you introduce to help promote your family life?
3. Which routines do you need to ditch?

DECIDING WHAT MATTERS

I read a story about a man who was extremely strict with his daughter and reprimanded her for the smallest thing.

It didn't make for a great father and daughter relationship.

One day she arrived late for breakfast and he was really annoyed with her. Instead of greeting her he exclaimed, "You child of the devil!"

Her reply was, "Morning, Father."

When I was about five years old I remember receiving a set of red foam boxing gloves from my own father. They were a Christmas gift and you would have thought he should have wanted to discourage fights between me and my older brother. But I guess boxing was seen as a sport five-year-olds should learn. Even Granny sat up late to watch the boxing on television. What is it about grannies and brute force violence? Anyway,

I wore the gloves but rarely picked a boxing match with my brother for two reasons.

Firstly, my brother was bigger than me. That tends to happen when brothers are four years older. A five-year-old pitched against a nine-year-old can only have one outcome and though my name was David, I had no faith in winning against some 'Goliath' of a brother.

Secondly, and perhaps more importantly, I didn't want to get hurt. You see, my little red foam gloves could inflict very little injury. Compare those with the full sized tough old leather boxing gloves my brother had passed down to him by Grandpa. Boy, they could really pack a punch. Though I complained my brother was rough with me, if he'd hit me with a boxing glove then that wasn't viewed as so bad and was fair game. Jolly hurt though.

Life isn't always a fair game, is it? Things go wrong and hurt, don't they? No matter how much we try to do the right thing we make mistakes. Why, only the other day I was explaining to my daughter, "Everyone makes mistakes and gets things wrong – especially your mother."

 DECIDING WHAT MATTERS

You see, the best we can be is human. To be perfectly human is to be a person who gets it 'wrong'. Sometimes we don't even realise when we get it wrong until someone 'kindly' points out our failings and we discover who our friends are!

And things get exaggerated, don't they? The smallest thing becomes a crisis and a crisis becomes Armageddon. The fly in the ointment isn't just a fly – it's a monster who hangs its arms over the side of the jar and stares menacingly right up at us.

If we adults make mistakes we can bet our children will. After all, we are the example they see every day. If we use bad language then our children will too. If we act dishonestly then we justify stealing to those who literally look up to us. I'm not suggesting dishonesty or swearing are merely mistakes (more like choices?) but that children learn from adults, are influenced greatly by us and possess the same ability to make some good decisions and some not so good ones. And, no matter how hard they try, they will make mistakes just like their parents too. It's inevitable though it doesn't mean we should give up on boundaries, consequences or helping children to develop character. I've found the most effective boundaries are those modelled and lived out by parents.

I'm not a naturally physically strong person (hence I never pursued boxing) and as a child I was extremely shy and withdrawn. Conflict for me was something to be avoided at all costs. As I got older, though, I learnt the importance of principles and that compromising is not always the right thing to do. Sometimes we have to stick to our guns and draw a line that we will not cross. Some things are personal choice while others are principles we'd probably all sign up to as important. And it's this difference that I think is key. If we're going to uncompromisingly stand our ground it better be over something that is important than over something that is trivial or a personal preference. Why? Because if we've any chance of making progress in the lives of our children it won't be by continual argument or control. The third lesson is this: *I will decide what's important and review the list regularly.*

This applies to so many things such as the boundaries you introduce, the moral code you teach and the flexibility you have to adapt as life moves on. Did you realise the 'rules' change as a child grows up? The boundaries you set in place for a two-year-old will change by the time they are five. And they'll be completely different when they're fifteen.

I have a confession to make. Really? Yes. I like watching Judge Judy. For those who have never watched her in action, she presides over a court in the US which televises the proceedings of small civil cases. Someone has a complaint and files it with the court. The other party then usually submits a counter claim and the disagreements seem to grow and grow.

What Judge Judy does is sift through all the ridiculous stuff and focus on what's important. She's uncompromising in her approach and no one is getting away with petty arguments or nonsense. She's fair and reaches a decision based on the evidenced facts. Her decision-making process makes for some interesting watching alone but there's something else I really like.

When questioning each party, Judge Judy often makes some comments about parental responsibilities and the teenage/young adult attitudes. She packs a punch to parents who take their kids to court and tells them they really ought to have sorted the mess out at home. To young adults living at home she's clear they must contribute to the family by applying for work and being responsible. To young teenagers she teaches them a lesson or two about respect. She's a straight talker and I love that. In all the shows I've watched I've never heard her award a judgement because of a trivial matter. It has to be 'big enough' or important enough or the case is dismissed. Great lesson for us all. Now, what would it be like if she visited and presided over our family disagreements?

I have to admit that looking back there have been times when my demands have been trivial, unreasonable or just lack insight into a situation. We've all probably been there. What I've found helpful with my teenage children is to decide what's important for their adult lives. What boundaries and 'non-negotiable' standards will help them become responsible adults? These are things I will choose to stand my ground over. Other things I accept as personal choice and probably not what I should be arguing about. The sort of things I think are important may be different from yours because of how we were raised or our cultural diversity. However, being able to sort out the priorities and what really matters is, in my view, an important part of parenting. You're going to want to know what's on my 'important' list aren't you? It could be longer than this book! It's not, but if I list a few you have to promise to think through them for yourself. Don't just take my list and make it law. It has to be adjusted for age and ability. What I have kept on the list now relates to teenagers and not toddlers. The younger the child the more things on the list there are that relate to their safety and learning.

Here's some items (in no particular order) that I think are important. What are yours?

- Study or work – doing nothing with your life is not an option and that may mean that between jobs you volunteer or help out at home or study again.
- Home is a place of safety. Do not bring in anything that may spoil this like drugs, weapons or people of poor reputation.
- You must contribute financially to the home when you earn so be responsible and offer to do this without being asked.

- Be open and honest. If something is troubling you remember we all love you and share it if you can. You don't have to suffer alone.
- Help around the home - it's your home too so be considerate and don't leave everything to someone else.
- Tell us what you 'need' and we'll do our best to help you. What you 'want' might not always be possible.
- Say what you feel and we'll try to understand and not judge. Keep talking to us about stuff.
- If you're going out please tell us where you are and what time you'll be home so we know you are okay. Call us if anything changes.
- Be respectful to everyone.
- Be kind – don't fight those who love you.
- Have fun and laugh.

One last story for you about boundaries. I know that teenagers can pose the greatest challenge to so many parents and carers so here's something to remind us that when we experience a boundary being pushed or an instruction being unfairly

 DECIDING WHAT MATTERS

challenged there are sometimes several different ways to achieve compliance. And they don't all have to include conflict.

There was an old man in Florida who owned a piece of land and a lovely house. He'd lived there for many years and in one secluded area there was a pond with shady banks, lush grass and tall trees. The water in the pond was inviting on a hot day and the local kids would walk by and long to swim in the pond.

But the old man was insistent that no one should be allowed to swim in the pond. He told people it was dangerous to swim in the pond and he erected a fence and signs which read, "Keep Out!" and "No Swimming!". The man regularly walked down to the pond to check no one was there and the kids always moved away from the fence when they saw him coming.

One hot day the man took a trip across town and a group of teenagers decided they'd climb over the fence and take a swim. They all ignored the signs and scaled the fence in their swimming costumes. They dipped their toes in the cool water and savoured the moment — they'd waited for this opportunity for a long time. Well, it wasn't long before there were six teenagers splashing and having fun in the pond. It was great. It was so great that they forgot the time and didn't notice the old man had returned. In fact, they didn't notice him walking towards the pond until he was standing at the bank.

The children stopped and looked at him in silence. One boy then shouted at him, "Well I suppose you're gonna tell us to get out, aren't you? We'll we're not gonna do what you say!"

The old man smiled and replied, "No, I'm not going to tell you to do anything. I've just come down to feed the alligator." The pond soon became empty of kids.

 DECIDING WHAT MATTERS

MIND CURVING QUESTIONS

1. If some rules are unspoken how can any child know what they are?
2. Which rules make sense and which ones will you introduce or drop?
3. Why do you need these rules?

THE PERSONALITY TEST

 # THE PERSONALITY TEST

I must be the only person who has failed a personality test. It seems like an impossible achievement but somehow I managed to pull it off and successfully score a zero with flying colours.

Let me explain. Personality tests have been widely used by companies when hiring staff to determine what 'sort' of person has come for interview and to assist in matching a personality type with a job role the company wishes to fill. Though I understand they can be useful I think they are flawed. Okay, I admit I'm probably biased in this view because I managed to fail one but taking a test to discover the 'real you' has to be risky, doesn't it?

A UK company once (and only once!) invited me to attend an interview because it seemed my technical skills matched perfectly with the job specifications they had advertised. What personality had to do with writing computer code I'll never be convinced about but I was sat at a desk with a set of fifty questions and told to take a pen and mark the answers to various statements by ticking a box. The possible answers were:

- Strongly agree
- Agree
- Neither agree or disagree
- Disagree
- Strongly disagree

Now, at the beginning of the test I was reassured that there were no wrong answers – just answer the questions as I saw fit. Great! I love tests where there are no wrong answers! If only school examinations were like this.

However, once I started to answer the statements it became apparent that it wasn't quite what I expected. Most of the statements related to whether or not I agreed with something relating to my reaction to a situation or an emotional response. Being someone who naturally analyses questions to the nth degree meant I found myself selecting the middle answer for every question. Sometimes I agreed with the statement but then again it depended on the situation so I might not agree with it all the time. Since I didn't agree or

 THE PERSONALITY TEST

disagree I chose, 'Neither agree nor disagree'. I felt this was a balanced answer and showed I had given proper thought and consideration to the statement.

I completed the test and moved on to the second part of the interview process. This involved a face-to-face interview with a manager. He introduced himself and just as we were about to discuss my application the personnel officer entered the room and stated that the interview had to end. I asked why and was told in no uncertain terms that I had scored zero in the personality test. They had never come across this before and were unable to ascertain if I had a personality. I assured them I did have one but they refused to believe me! I suggested they interview me and discuss my answers but again they refused. I had failed the unfailable test.

I often look back on this experience with great amusement but it does raise another question about the organisation who interviewed me. Why couldn't they determine my personality by talking with me and getting to know me face-to-face? You see, what really matters is not so much personality but character. I can be fun meeting an outgoing jovial person but if they're a dishonest liar and a cheat you'd want to think twice about employing them.

This leads nicely on to a lesson parents do well to remember: *I will nurture good character because good character matters.* When we raise our children, they will have a personality. It will naturally develop and mature over the years. They may be quiet and thoughtful, pensive and deliberating. They may be loud and extroverted, rash and decisive. Neither are wrong – just different. They could be a mixture depending on the situation. However, I have noted that society tends to lean towards the extrovert when it comes to favourites despite the fact that it seems to be the quieter people who bring about real change in the world. Those who shout loudest may push their way into the limelight but it isn't always the best way. You see, personality is one thing but character is quite another. Character is built by the experience and input of those around us as well as from our own experience. Making choices to be honest and truthful despite the personal cost takes courage and more than a popular happy-go-lucky type of personality. Good character means I buckle up rather than buckle under.

 # THE PERSONALITY TEST

My father always advocated being honest because it meant he could sleep at night. He's right. Convenient truth is not the same as honesty because an uncompromising man or woman has been created by the sound investment of parents who have good character. When we raise our children we'd better make sure we focus on ensuring they understand that knowing and being who they are is more important than following popular flawed opinion. Making the choice to do what's right takes guts and determination. Good character encompasses all these things – personality doesn't. And one day we'll face a test.

MIND CURVING QUESTIONS

1. Who in society has character which you admire?
2. What is it about their character that you admire?
3. How will you teach your child about good character?
4. If there was one characteristic you would like your child to master, what would it be?

LETTING GO

 LETTING GO

A large commercial jet was making the journey from London to Singapore. It was full of passengers and about an hour into the journey a voice was heard over the loud speaker system. "Welcome aboard the world's first pilotless flight. Things have changed and everything is being controlled by a super-computer. There is no co-pilot or navigator as they are no longer needed.

Everything, from take-off to landing, is being achieved electronically so sit back, let go and enjoy the ride. We are travelling at 35,000 feet but please do not worry. Nothing can

go wrong...

go wrong...

go wrong...

go wrong...

go wrong."

One day parents wake up with the realisation that their children are young adults. They've become more knowledgeable with technology (how incredibly infuriating is it when we can't fix something but they can?) and maybe start to show they are more intelligent, more witty and curious. They even start to have opinions! We feel like they are beginning to have the upper hand and maybe they've already begun to decide which care home we should retire to (better start being extra nice to them, I suppose). But stop. Wait! Hold on there just a moment.

Time may have whizzed by for us but it hasn't for them. They're just starting out and they still need us. In fact, they'll need us for quite some time but maybe in a slightly different capacity. Let me explain.

At the time of writing this very text I'm fifty-one years old and my children remind me I was born

 LETTING GO

just twenty-two years after the Second World War (witty huh?). I no longer feel twenty-one and when I look at my children I no longer see them as helpless kids totally dependent on me. The blonde fluffy curly hair has been replaced by straight long hair and makeup (I refer to my youngest daughter, not my eldest son). The relationship has changed and friendship becomes part of the equation. I see less of them (but I think of them every day) because one has a flat, another is studying and another is out and about seeing friends. The fourth spends much of her time with homework, texting friends or watching football. Their lives are changing and so is the nature of our relationship.

I'll always be their dad and I'll always choose to love them. There is, though, a mutual respect that comes about from their ability to make their own decisions and choices that are based on good character. There's kind of an equality of contribution into the relationship. Okay, so they still leave their bedroom in a mess but they are more considerate when it comes to how their mum might think or what will make her feel loved and appreciated. That comes about because they are making grown-up choices based on the example mum and dad have shown and the principles we've applied when raising them. They are discovering that mum and dad matter to them not just because they provide a roof over their head, food on the table and a comfy bed to sleep in. They matter, well, because they're mum and dad. They love us.

Now, I know we're really fortunate. We have a nice home and a good relationship with our kids (though we've been through some tough things together). Not everyone has that and I recognise people's personal circumstances are different. But what I'm trying to share here is that as children become young adults the relationship changes. That leads me on to examine our response. Now that the banana is really turning, what do we choose to do about it?

When it comes to parenting there are many essential ingredients we can identify that are crucial when raising children. There's the undisputed need for a commitment to love, a programme of nurturing boundaries to keep them safe, discipline to learn what really matters and the development of a character that holds strong even during the tough times. These are the foundations which make the last lesson easier.

 # LETTING GO

Though there are many ingredients there's probably only one serious destination a parent needs to head for. You know what it is? The journey to freedom. One day our children must live their own lives. They have to make their own choices and decisions without us. The day must come when, in their own way, our child no longer asks what they should do but is able instead to tell us what they are going to do. That marks a point when a parent can say, "I've done a great job."

We want our children to be free but we know that entails handing over responsibility of their lives to them and letting go. The thing is, they're just not quite ready and neither are we. Yet, letting go is so important. That's my fifth lesson - *I will practice letting go as they grow.*

I say *practice* because it's not straightforward. The fifteen-year-old that wants to take on the world knows next to nothing about life experience and responsibility. They think they know what's best for them and that we are holding them back from a big adventure. What makes things even more challenging is the fact that 'their friends' are allowed out to parties all night so they shouldn't even have to ask. All night parties? I can barely stay awake beyond 10pm. So, do I need to be concerned? You bet. Late night parties are a place to experiment with new freedoms — some okay and some not so okay. The trick here is to educate, state the boundaries and be in the annoying position to say, "I told you so."

I'm simply not prepared to completely let go because children need to learn, I need to practice letting go and they have to prove trustworthiness. Remember what I said about developing character? If character is lacking then so will the ability to make grown-up decisions. They will swim with the tide and just go with the flow. That's why lifeguard parents are essential. We need to love by staying close and ensuring we can always see them while they are learning to swim without the water wings.

Once children are able to demonstrate an ability to make decisions to keep themselves safe parents can let go of those areas where experience has proved it's okay to step back. That doesn't mean we let go of everything else — it's a gradual process. However, we must have their freedom as our goal. Why? Because we shouldn't decide to control our children's lives forever.

 # LETTING GO

At fifty I thought I'd reached a pretty important milestone. My children had all but grown up and left home and I was getting used to the idea of more space. What I hadn't counted on was the news that I was to become a grandfather. And not just once – twice!

At fifty? I'm not complaining, just a little surprised that time has passed so quickly and the next generation is poised to take over. My parents must think I have it easy – they're great grandparents and on my wife's side some have become great great grandparents. Five generations.

The thing is, I don't see my daughters as grown up women – they're still my girls. All the principles above still apply only they now extend to encouraging my girls to decide to adopt them with their own children. How? By demonstrating them in my relationship with my grandchildren. That does mean regressing to a young person again with energy and enthusiasm! Actually, I may have over done it the other week when my daughter messaged my wife following an evening of babysitting. "Why is my son so hyper? Did you give him chocolate or something?"

"No, he had too much of grandad," was the reply.

I'll be honest with you. This whole grandparent thing feels kind of strange. It's like I'm becoming obsolete while at the same time stepping into a role as senior figure to give reassurance and advice. To the child I'm a source of entertainment!

There are special relationships to build with some new children. But they're not mine. My emotions are very mixed because I know life is changing rapidly and I'm learning to adjust again. Maybe it's true that when your children leave home you regain some time and space. But I wasn't really looking for that or wishing for it. It just happened. You turn your back for a few moments and they've all grown up. Next thing they'll be looking through care home magazines... I'm off!

Sometimes letting go is a process we gradually introduce and sometimes it's forced upon us by circumstances. Sometimes we have to encourage our children to swim and at other times we have to cut the line because they are struggling so hard that the rope burns our hands. But though the latter experience may leave us with the scars or

 **LETTING GO**

pain we follow on and look out for them because long ago we made that decision to love.

MIND CURVING QUESTIONS

1. How can you loosen your grip?
2. How are you going to help your child towards freedom?
3. What will you do to enable your child to stay close to you even when they have gone?

 IN SUMMARY

IN SUMMARY...

 **IN SUMMARY**

Here are the five lessons again.

1. **I will choose to love my child because that is what is always needed.**
2. **I will introduce routine and consistency as soon as I can.**
3. **I will decide what's important and review the list regularly.**
4. **I will nurture good character because good character matters.**
5. **I will practice letting go as they grow.**

 FINAL THOUGHT

FINAL THOUGHT – STOP LOOKING OVER THE FENCE

 FINAL THOUGHT

I was recently helping a group of students with some research they were conducting as part of their PhD studies. It had been quite a long run of tests and experiments and I was allowed to take a break. I remember one student coming up to me and asking, "So what is your condition or problem? You seem quite normal to me."

I was very tempted to reply with the words, "Well, that's reassuring to know. I guess that's why they let me out into the community."

Have you ever wondered sometimes what people mean when they use the term 'normal'? I know I have. What on earth are they describing? Who decides what 'normal' is and where or when it applies? Are there cultural standards or is there a worldwide fixed measurement? You see, *I can't squeeze with ease into the mould we've been sold.* Why? I'm a little different from everyone else. I think differently and I find certain environments more challenging to carry out simple tasks (I'm not referring to breathing under water!). I'm different because I have an autistic mind which gives me a huge advantage over others in the field of analysis but some challenges with social interaction. Some have asked whether I consider myself as having a label – "Are you autistic or do you have autism? How would you like us to refer to you?" My preference is to be referred to by my name! But I'm not offended by being asked. Why? Because I'd prefer it if people asked questions and were inquisitive rather than just judged without understanding.

Now, I'm different but not abnormal. I'm socially challenged but not devoid of an amazing ability. To me, I'm normal because normal is that we are all different. Diversity is what makes the world such an amazing place. And guess what, normal does quite often change from one culture to another culture, within countries, communities and also within families. There really is no true 'normal' or predetermined fixed state of personality or

 # FINAL THOUGHT

behaviour to which everyone in the world must aspire.

So, why do schools or societies try and make everyone the same? Why are families so keen to have everything just right? Remember the last time you knew of someone who gave birth? What is it that people invariably say - "Is everything okay?" It's kind of an unconscious hope that mum is well and that the baby has nothing 'wrong' with him or her. It disregards the many families who choose to continue with a pregnancy even though they know the child has a disability and will be 'different'. Bringing children into the world is a risk.

I've read about techniques to try and 'cure' children of autism. They centre on trying to ensure the child acts like everyone else. But the truth is, what is going on in the inside can't be 'cured'. I may try and behave like everyone else but that only lasts a while and can be tiring. I certainly cannot change who I am and I don't want to. And guess what, I'm not going to try. I don't need to be cured – I'm not a piece of bacon. In fact, if you took away my autistic mind my contribution to the world could be less and that matters a great deal to me.

I'm an advocate for raising children with autistic minds to grow up and be themselves, their brains intact and less warped by a society's social expectations. That doesn't mean someone should become the 'label' others give them but I'm far happier seeing a child become an adult with strategies to help rather than a standard 'normality' to become. Sometimes their behaviour is a way to regulate their emotions so trying to stop the behaviour may only make things worse for them. Not all behaviour is 'bad' - sometimes it's just behaviour. Just as I had difficulties in childhood trying to adjust so did many other autistically minded people in history – Albert Einstein, Isaac Newton, Michelangelo, Alan Turing – and yet their contribution as adults may well have only been possible because they were different.

I've used autism as an example but you could look at many other things which may cause a child to learn and develop in different ways from other children (ADHD, OCD, dyslexia, sensory processing disorder, partial sight). What children need is help and adjustment in the way they are taught in school or supported as people rather than being squeezed into a mould to try and become like

 FINAL THOUGHT

everyone else. The opportunity to achieve should be based not on whether our children can conform or lose an impairment. Opportunity is rightfully theirs to take up and achieve in their own way. Being real is important but pointing out their deficits or encouraging them to become a label is far less helpful than extolling their abilities, talents, interests and identity - even though it won't make them like everyone else.

Something else I've noticed hasn't changed over the years and it's most unhelpful. Parents compare their children with other children. Ever heard it going on in the pub, school playground, parent's evenings, social events or just in the street? One parent tends to come away feeling smaller, more guilty, discouraged or unhappy. This happens even though they have invested so much love, care, attention and time into their child's life. They should feel uplifted, encouraged and full of hope because in reality they have actually been good parents. Perhaps these sorts of discussions should be avoided.

Just because someone's grown-up child has a 'high-flying' career in the city (it can be a long way down if they crash) doesn't mean a parent cannot be proud of their child who has adjusted with a disability to secure voluntary work for a charity. You may wish for more for your child but you don't need to feel you have failed as a parent - you haven't. Your priorities for your son or daughter don't have to be the same as everyone else's. Some focus on education, some on careers and some on happiness or community contribution. Your child is an individual.

I've got to tell you that my family life can seem like a rollercoaster ride. I don't have it all mapped out to take the smooth straight route because I just can't find one. My wife asked me once whether we were bad parents because there are so many challenges for our children even though we've tried to point them in the 'right' direction (whatever that is!).

I understood her heartfelt concern because we've faced so many situations. Yet my reply was a definite "No". How can I be so confident or reassuring? Because even when things go horribly wrong we are both there to love, support, direct and help them. Parenting is less about perfection and more about perseverance. It's 5% luck and 95% effort! You can't control everything because

 FINAL THOUGHT

control isn't the goal. Helping our children towards freedom and independence from us is where we're heading. I say 'from us' because the hope is they will outlive us and make their own choices. They may still need support from others but being able to continue in this world without us is important.

One of my favourite films is 'The Best of Men'. It tells the story of how a German-born British neurologist called Dr Ludwig Guttmann established the Paralympic Games in England. He battled with the medical establishment, prejudices, a lack of staff and equipment and the unbelief of his own military paraplegic patients. He persevered to help each patient regain purpose and dignity after injuries sustained on the battlefields of the Second World War. What he worked towards has always reminded me that everyone of us is unique and has a life to live where we should, as far as possible, make our own choices. Towards the end of the film Private William Heath asks Dr Guttmann what he should do. The reply is memorable. "William, I cannot help you. Do not ask me what you should do. Tell me what you are going to do. Then I can help you."

Perhaps that sums up the final aim of a parent? Looking over the fence doesn't always help - so please come away. Resist unhealthy comparison and help your unique child to decide what they want to do and help them towards it. It's less about trying to straighten a banana and more about providing what is helpful and allowing it to grow in its own natural bendy way.

After all, a banana wouldn't be a banana if it wasn't curved, would it?

Can You Help?

If you've found this book helpful perhaps you'd like to tell your friends, colleagues and family about it because I'd love to encourage them too.

You might consider rating the book on Amazon.co.uk or putting a post on social media such as Facebook or Twitter. Your support will mean more people will be able to answer the question, "What should I know when raising children?"

STRAIGHTENING THE BANANA